MIKE BEYNON

BBC BOOKS

This book is dedicated to all the production team of
The Really Wild Show

The author wishes to acknowledge the help of
Hilary Jeffkins, Terry Nutkins, Nick Davies and Chris Packham
in the compilation of this book.

Published by BBC Books
A division of BBC Enterprises Ltd,
Woodlands, 80 Wood Lane, London W12 0TT

First published 1988
© Mike Beynon and the contributors 1988

ISBN 0 563 20636 5

Set in 10/12pt Helvetica by Ace Filmsetting Ltd, Frome, Somerset
Colour reproduction by Technik Ltd, Berkhamsted, Herts
Printed and bound in England by
Redwood Burn Ltd, Trowbridge, Wilts

CONTENTS

Presenters' introduction	**6**
Vroom, vroom	**8**
Jump!	**11**
Why does a peacock have such a big tail?	**12**
Dolphin rescue	**14**
Ron I: a superstar is born	**16**
The deepest bird in the world	**18**
Why are flamingos pink?	**19**
Butterfly bits	**20**
Ron II: just another day in the office	**24**
Pets: Dear Really Wild Show . . .	**28**
How did animals get invented?	**34**
Ron III: Dear Ron . . .	**37**
The commonest bird in Britain	**38**
The biggest leaf in the world	**39**
International wildlife photographer of the year	**40**
Animals in danger	**43**
Dinosaur facts	**48**
Return of the death star	**50**
I want to meet a koala	**52**
Ron IV: happy birthday Ron	**54**
The rarest bird in Britain	**56**
Panda page	**58**
The (second) biggest fish in the world	**60**
Stephen the chameleon	**62**
Ron IV: Ron's big night	**63**

Hi. I'm Terry Nutkins, and I want to welcome you to *The Really Wild Show*. Every year, we get thousands of letters from our viewers asking questions about animals. In this book, Nick, Chris and I aim to answer as many of those questions as possible, and to cram in a load of amazing facts as well. We'll be including extracts from your letters, and some of your super drawings.

Terry is the Director of Windsor Safari Park. Nowadays he's an important man in animal circles – but he started out at the age of only twelve, cleaning out the elephants at London Zoo. Later Terry became an expert in training dolphins and specialised in marine mammals, eventually becoming the manager of the dolphinarium at Woburn.

Terry's too shy to admit it, but he's received two awards for animal rescues. The first one was in 1984, when he helped to save a humpback whale that was caught up in a length of old metal cable off the coast of north-west Scotland. Terry dived for many hours, in cold and very dangerous conditions, to cut away the cable and free the whale. For that, he received a Silver Medal from the Scottish Society for the Prevention of Cruelty to Animals. And in 1986, the RSPCA awarded Terry a certificate of merit for his help in rescuing a wild dolphin trapped in the River Severn. You can read all about that rescue on page 14.

Like me, Nick loves sea mammals. She's even swum with sperm whales and blue whales off the coast of Sri Lanka – not to mention wild dolphins. But it's as an expert on bats that Nick has become known on *The Really Wild Show* – in particular, the greater horseshoe bat.

Chris is nuts about bird-watching. And he's very knowledgeable. There aren't many people who can catch him out when it comes to facts about British birds. His favourite is the red-backed shrike – the butcher bird. The shrike is Britain's rarest breeding bird and, as you can read on page 56, Chris has been involved for years in protecting it from egg thieves.

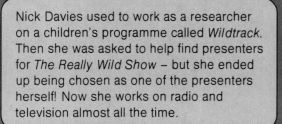

Nick Davies used to work as a researcher on a children's programme called *Wildtrack*. Then she was asked to help find presenters for *The Really Wild Show* – but she ended up being chosen as one of the presenters herself! Now she works on radio and television almost all the time.

Now Chris here really has talent. Not only is he a television presenter, he's also a still photographer, a film cameraman, a writer and a poet. Chris has won awards as Wildlife Photographer of the Year. He's also made two half-hour films in the series *A Day in the Life* . . . In one of these films about a family of kestrels, Chris filmed the young kestrel chicks on the nest through a hole cut in the back of a tree. And in another sequence, he filmed from a microlight aircraft to give an idea of what it's like to be a kestrel in flight.

NICK   **TERRY**   **CHRIS**

THE FASTEST MAMMAL in the world, on land, is the cheetah. It can reach 50 miles per hour (mph). But it can only keep up this speed for a very short time, because it uses up so much energy. This means that cheetahs have to be fairly sure of killing their prey before they set off on a high-speed hunt. If they chase and then fail to kill, it will be a long time before they build up enough energy to hunt again.

THE FASTEST SNAKE in the world is probably the black mamba, which can go as fast as 10 mph.

THE FASTEST SEA MAMMAL in the world is probably the killer whale, with speeds of up to 34 mph.

THE FASTEST FISH in the world is the sail-fish, which can reach over 60 mph. Sailfish look rather like swordfish. They have a very long upper jaw, a bit like a sword, and a very large dorsal fin.

A hippopotamus can run faster than a man. Two hippos have been recorded as running at 30 mph.

A roadrunner is a bird that seldom flies, but it can run very fast – at about 15 mph – with its short wings outstretched.

Ostriches are the largest living birds. They are flightless, but have powerful legs which make it possible for them to run at more than 30 mph.

BRITISH
CHAMPIONS
—— in the ——
SPEED STAKES

Yes, there are at least two British world champio speedsters, who've starred on *The Really Wil Show.*

THE FASTEST SPIDER IN THE WORLI
The world's fastest spider is an animal you mig well find in your bathroom. Its proper name *Tegenaria gigantica*, but it's more often called t common house spider. Its large body, short le and fast, scuttling running often gives mums a

dads the screaming heebie-jeebies. But you lot know it's a hundred times more frightened of us than we are of it. Anyway, it's very interesting – it's a world record holder.

In the last series, we brought some record-holding *Tegenaria* into the studio and raced them down a one-metre track. We made the far end very dark because spiders run fastest when they're heading for the safety of the shadows. Spiders' legs are hydraulic – they use blood pressure to pump their legs forward, and muscle power to pull them back. But they can only keep up a fast speed for very short bursts, because, unlike us, they don't have a very efficient breathing system. The more active spiders don't even have lungs – just tubes which run from openings on the outside of their bodies, taking oxygen directly to the tissues.

Anyway, Terry timed the *Tegenaria* at just over a second and a half over a metre track, which works out at 1.49 mph – a world record!

THE FASTEST BIRD IN THE WORLD

There's a lot of controversy about this one. The spine-tailed swift has often been called the fastest bird, but experts now believe that speeds of 70 mph or so for this bird have been wildly exaggerated. We think that the fastest bird in the world in *level* flight is a duck – our own British eider duck. In steady level flight the eider has been recorded at 48 mph. Eiders can fly so fast because, although they have only short wings, they have huge breast muscles which provide the power for fast flight. The second fastest in level flight is the Bewick swan – another British species – which can reach 45 mph.

But the fastest bird of all must be a bird of prey – not when it's flying straight and level, but when it's diving out of the sky at its prey in what falconers call a *stoop.* And the fastest of these is reckoned to be our own peregrine falcon. But here again, experts argue about how fast it's actually going in a stoop. The only thing for me to do was to find out for myself.

So, especially for *The Really Wild Show*, the Scottish police lent us a radar speed gun which they use to detect speeding motorists. One very cold winter's day up in Sutherland, I set out with falconer Stephen Franks and his peregrine falcon.

We sent the bird off in the worst possible conditions – driving snow, and bitterly cold and windy. The peregrine climbed to 300 metres before Stephen threw out a lure. The bird folded back its wings and dropped out of the sky like a silver bullet. I held the radar gun trained right at the bird as it dived at an incredible speed towards the ground. It's impossible to explain how the peregrine manages to pull out of such an incredible dive without tearing itself apart. I'm sure an aeroplane would have torn its wings off.

But the peregrine, of course, was perfectly all right and when I examined the radar gun afterwards, I found it had registered a maximum speed of 96 mph.

Stephen was certain that under better conditions the peregrine could go faster – up to 120 mph. This is still nowhere near the 200 mph that has been claimed in the past. But even so, that makes our peregrine not only the fastest bird in the world, but also the fastest moving animal of all!

JUMP!

German Shepherd • Highest 3·5m

Kangaroo Highest 3·2m Longest 12·8 m

Greyhound Longest 9·1m

Salmon • Longest 3·7 m

Bushbaby • Longest 2m

Flea • Highest 197mm Longest 330mm

Salmon do their enormous leaps when they're heading up river to spawn, jumping rocks and other obstacles in their path. Kangaroos use their hind legs like enormous pogo sticks. Fellow Australian bushbabies leap up to 2 metres from branch to branch. German Shepherd dogs hold one high jump record, but that's for a leap and climb over a scramble board. But, without a shadow of a doubt, the champion jumper is the flea. On *The Really Wild Show* Nick measured a cat flea jumping 28 cm – that's 140 times its own length. And it's reckoned that a flea can take off with an acceleration 140 times greater than that of an Apollo moon rocket.

WHY DOES A PEACOCK

It's magnificent, isn't it, the peacock's enormous tail? Over a hundred long feathers, each with a huge eye-spot, shimmering with colour. And it's at its most magnificent when raised in an enormous fan, and then made to quiver so that it sounds like the wind rustling through the trees. It's stunning, breath-taking – but what's it all for?

Well, for a start it's not a tail at all. You can see the real tail if you look at the peacock from behind – it's those feathers in the shape of a small shield that support and spread the larger feathers of the train.

Most zoologists agree that the size of a peacock's fan is all to do with courtship – male birds attracting females to mate with them. The peacock is a bird of paradise and, as a rule, male birds of paradise are brightly coloured with very eye-catching feathers and they perform very elaborate dances and displays. The female, however, is usually rather dull. But from that point onwards everybody disagrees.

Some people say the peacock's train is an advertisement – the more colourful and impressive it is, the more likely females are to choose him. Another theory is that the train is so big and heavy that any peacock strong enough to carry it must be a mate worth having.

But there's a recent theory that I really like and it's all to do with hypnotism. Just look at those enormous 'eye-spots' in the train. In that huge area of shimmering, iridescent colour, they stand out as the only solid points. Stare at one, and the black centre looks like the pupil of an eye surrounded by the deep blue or emerald of the iris. These eyes seem to draw you in, make you stare, make you go all woozy – in short, they almost hypnotise you. At least, that's the theory. It certainly made me feel funny on the day we took these peacock pictures at Rode Bird Garden. And the theory goes on to say, the bigger the train, the bigger the eyes. And the bigger the eyes, the more powerful they will be at attracting a peahen.

But anybody who owns or understands peafowl knows that this fantastic display by the cock is more often than not totally ignored by the hen bird. Certainly, this peacock's display had a lot more effect on me than on the peahen. She just wasn't impressed.

HAVE SUCH A BIG TAIL?

DOLPHIN

The 11th of September 1986 began with a phone call from the RSPCA. They were very worried about a dolphin that had swum up the River Severn and had apparently been there some time. They wanted my advice on what to do, and asked if I would mind coming along and having a look.

The dolphin was in a part of the River Severn that was totally unknown to me. As I got closer, I found I was driving along narrow lanes which seemed to be taking me deeper into the country – certainly not an area where I would expect to find a sea mammal.

When I eventually arrived, I was introduced to the Severn Auxiliary Rescue Association. I explained to them that I wanted to get a closer look at the dolphin and so we headed out in their rubber inflatable. I felt an incredible surge of excitement and wonder, when I caught my first close glimpse of the animal. It was indeed a dolphin and not a porpoise as I had thought it might have been. Common dolphins, of which this was one, are just one of the nine species around the British coast. They range right across the Atlantic Ocean and live in groups of thirty or so, hunting herring, mackerel and squid to a depth of 40 metres as they swim the seas.

This animal was swimming very strongly and by its behaviour it had obviously been eating well. However, dolphins are sea mammals and I could only hope that this one would not be suffering from any skin infections caused by having lived in fresh water for a number of weeks.

Catching a dolphin in a wide river isn't easy, although there was no shortage of suggestions from well-meaning people. "Why not use a net?" some people said. I wasn't keen on this idea. The dolphin could quite easily panic, swim into the net, get tangled up and drown. I eventually decided that we would try to catch her the next day, by just jumping in and grabbing her.

I really would have liked to have caught her there and then, but the whole operation would need very careful planning. I would need boats and vans at the ready along with a dolphin sling, vaseline and lanolin for her skin, and plenty of foam for her to rest on once she was out of the water. Also a wet suit for myself to keep out some of the cold!

I contacted Paul Appleby at the production office of *The Really Wild Show*, just to let him know what I was up to. Paul was concerned when I told him about the dolphin. He told me that amongst the letters from viewers in *The Really Wild Show* office, there was one from a young boy called Todd Williams who desperately wanted to meet a wild dolphin; and Paul wondered whether I could take him along with me.

The next day I headed back down the M4 to Longney with Steve and Dave from Windsor Safari Park. There we met up with Paul, the *Really Wild Show* film crew and Todd Williams. Todd was a

RESCUE

wonderful lad and he was every bit as concerned about the dolphin as I was.

I had made up my mind what to do and I did not want to waste any time. I had to catch her at the first attempt. Dolphins are intelligent animals and she would soon realise what I was up to if I didn't succeed the first time.

Experts go to aid of a dolphin in distress

Steve and I quickly put on our wet suits and flippers. The current was just a little bit too strong for us to swim, so we used an inflatable boat to get close to the dolphin and then gently manoeuvred her to shallower water. Over the years I have spent a great deal of time in the water with dolphins and I instinctively knew the right time to attempt the catch. I leapt into the water, swam behind her and grabbed hold of her just in front of the dorsal fin. She struggled for only just a few seconds, then gave in. I first noticed her eyes – she seemed to have an inner calmness and certainly did not seem at all frightened or distressed. Steve and I lifted her on board the inflatable – she must have weighed at least 56 kilos – and headed for the shore at high speed.

We laid the dolphin on a foam mattress and I took a close look at her. She was very fat and very inquisitive, her eyes darting from one person to another, but happily she was not struggling. There was no physical damage, although her skin was flaking quite badly. I felt that she knew we were trying to help. Dolphins are very strong, and she could have put up a tremendous fight if she had wanted to.

We carried her over to the waiting van and lifted her into it, being very gentle so as to avoid her tail flukes being grazed or catching on anything. The RSPCA officers were in the front seats and Todd and I in the back with the dolphin, along with *The Really Wild Show* cameraman and soundman.

Once Todd had got over his initial wonder he wanted to know everything. "Is it OK, Terry? Where does it breathe? Will it be all right?" he asked me. I reassured him and we then covered her skin with vaseline and lanolin to keep it in good condition and stop it from cracking, and we sprayed her with water to keep her cool.

I suppose it must have taken $2\frac{1}{2}$ hours to travel the 60 miles to Barry Docks but, as always when you want to get somewhere in a hurry, the journey seemed endless. The last hurdle was to carry our dolphin down two flights of very narrow, winding stairs at the end of the pier. This took some time but we managed it smoothly. Puffing and panting, we eventually got her on board the Barry Docks Pilot Boat, which had been standing by, patiently awaiting our arrival.

We headed out of Barry and started to prepare for the canvas sling to be lifted over the side with the dolphin safely wrapped in it. She still seemed very calm and alert, and her breathing was quite steady considering how long she had been out of the water. Dolphins tend to get stiff if they are kept out of the water for any length of time, and so I got ready to go in the water with her to help if necessary.

Once I was in the water I could feel the current tugging at me; the deck of the boat seemed a long way up. The crew, and indeed everyone on board, gently lifted the dolphin over the side of the boat and lowered her down to me. Todd was now looking on with a concerned expression. When the dolphin reached the water I started to move the canvas sling away from her body and, as I expected, she needed a few seconds to acclimatise herself again. I kept her blowhole above the water until I felt her starting to move forwards. Within seconds she was moving out of the sling and into the deep salty water. I took one last look at her eyes, but she didn't see me. She was too busy going home.

BY TERRY NUTKINS

A SUPERSTAR

The first ever programme of *The Really Wild Show* is broadcast to a studio audience of hundreds, and a television audience of millions. The stars of the show – Terry, Chris and Nick – nervously bask in their new-found fame, little knowing they are about to be joined by an as-yet-unknown nobody. A mere spider. An animal despised, feared and loathed by most people. But Ron is about to change all that.

It all started because Marc Shedden, a young lad from Cardigan in Wales, wrote in asking if he could hold a tarantula. Terry got hold of a Mexican red-kneed tarantula and got it to walk onto Marc's hand right in the middle of the studio. Most people would have been frightened, but of course Marc and Terry thought it was wonderful. The camera zoomed in on the tarantula, showing its sleek body and beautiful bristles, soft to the touch but, as Marc said, a bit "tickly" as well.

In the studio control-room, there were murmurs of approval from the production team. Tough producers and directors, who'd seen it all before, were strangely affected by the elegance and beauty of the tarantula. In the audience, children were say-ing, "Please can I hold him too?"; and as soon as the recording finished, they rushed forward to be allowed to stroke him.

Suddenly people were realising that they weren't frightened of tarantulas at all; the very opposite, in fact. "Isn't he sweet?" they said. "Isn't he attractive?" Ron had started to work his magic.

Rumour has it that Ron got his name when a bored producer, walking into the wrong studio and finding himself face to face with a tarantula, shouted, "Strike me! It's a monster spider! Run!" But the true story is now lost in the mists of time. All we know is that as the audience left the studio, they were all talking about Ron – the real star of the show. And that evening the first WE LOVE RON sticker appeared in his dressing room.

Nowadays Ron generously allows Terry, Nick and Chris to go on presenting *The Really Wild Show*, sure in the knowledge that *he* is the real star. He sees himself more as a spokesman for spider-dom, sweeping away centuries of fear and pre-judice. Few children are now afraid to touch him, and his fan mail grows every day. Says Ron, "It just

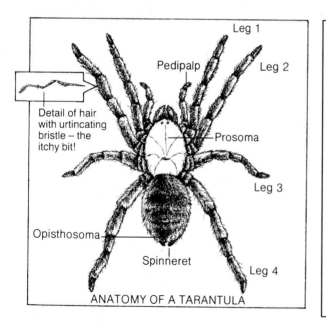

Leg 1

Pedipalp

Leg 2

Detail of hair with urtincating bristle – the itchy bit!

Prosoma

Leg 3

Opisthosoma

Spinneret

Leg 4

ANATOMY OF A TARANTULA

• PASSPORT •

NAME
Ron Red Knee but full name is *Brachypelma smithi*.

NATIONALITY
North American – Mexican.

OCCUPATION
Television personality.

DATE OF BIRTH
Uncertain but officially Feb. 17.

RON – PERSONAL DETAILS

....*DATELINE: Tuesday January 21 1986*...

IS BORN

goes to show that it's grown-ups, not children, who are afraid of spiders. And children pick up these fears. I'm out to prove that spiders are interesting, even lovable animals – and if anybody tells you otherwise, then *they're* the wimps!''

SEX
Ron may well be a Ronnette! Male and female tarantulas are similar in appearance but females are far more common.

RESIDENCE
Mexico – *'Burrow'*. Females live in underground burrows that consist of a tube-like entrance with a chamber at the end. All that can be seen from the outside is a small round hole about the size of a tenpence piece. Males on the other hand don't tend to live in burrows and just wander around.
Britain – *'Aquarium'*. A tank with cork chips, bark, a water dish and plenty of food.

DISTINGUISHING MARKS
Slightly bald at bottom. Tarantulas use their back legs to flick hairs off their abdomens. These hairs, called urticating bristles, are shaped like tiny harpoons and have an irritating chemical on them. They are used to scare away enemies and can be a very itchy experience. Ron also has eight eyes!

SPECIAL STATUS
CITES: appendix II. Now officially recognised as an "endangered" species. Trade now severely restricted. Each red-kneed tarantula brought out of Mexico must have a permit. But spiders already in this country do not have to be returned. So Ron is a legal alien, permanently resident abroad

Usual signature

TIME: 4.30 pm.... EVENT: BBC-1 Television....

❝❝Birds outside? We are 265 metres under the sea! Do you take me for a fool, mein Kapitän?!❞❞

It's no joke. There really are birds flying around at vast depths under the sea. Actually, of course, they're not flying but swimming, since these birds are penguins. A group of emperor penguins was once recorded at an incredible depth of 265 metres.

Their wings aren't so much wings as flippers, and they move them when submerged as though they're flying under water. They also have a thick layer of fat, rather like a waterproof overcoat, which stops them from freezing. But scientists still don't understand how it is that emperor penguins can dive to such depths, and stay under water for 15 minutes or more, and yet not suffer from "the bends" when they surface.

The Deepest Bird in the World

WHY ARE FLAMINGOS PINK?

If you look at a flamingo's mouth, you'll see that it's shaped in a very funny way – like a sort of scoop. In fact it works like a filter, and with it the flamingo sieves out tiny little creatures – crustaceans – from the water. These crustaceans contain blue-green algae which have a pigment (colouring) in them, like the one in carrots and tomatoes; and it is this pigment that turns the flamingo pink.

We wouldn't go pink if *we* ate those algae, because it's the way the flamingo digests its food that makes it go this colour. The pigment in the algae is actually poisonous in large quantities, and so to get rid of it, the flamingo puts the pink colouring in its feathers.

• FLAMINGO FACT •

Flamingos' knees aren't really their knees at all – they're their ankles!
They bend backwards when the flamingo sits down.

BUTTERFLY BITS

Queen Alexandra Birdwing   Monarchs   Swallowtail

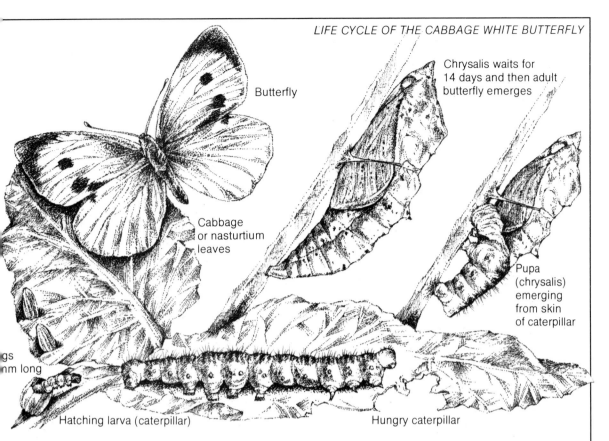

Butterfly

Chrysalis waits for 14 days and then adult butterfly emerges

Cabbage or nasturtium leaves

Pupa (chrysalis) emerging from skin of caterpillar

gs
nm long

Hatching larva (caterpillar)

Hungry caterpillar

The largest butterfly in the world is the Queen Alexandra birdwing. Its wings have an overall span of up to 280 mm. It lives in Papua New Guinea.

The largest butterfly ever seen in Britain is the monarch, also called the milkweed. It has a wing span of up to 106 mm. It's not really a British butterfly, however – just a very rare visitor. The monarch is found mostly in North America, and it migrates in vast numbers from as far north as Canada to as far south as Florida. It's possible that during this migration a few individuals may have been blown off course right across the Atlantic. More likely, though, the few British sightings are of monarchs which have come from the Canary Islands.

The largest resident butterfly in Britain is the swallowtail, now found only in the Norfolk Broads.

Its wing span measures up to 90 mm. It's a close relation of the massive birdwing butterflies of South-East Asia. It's a protected species in Britain.

How long does it take a caterpillar to change into a butterfly?

Caterpillars don't change straight into butterflies, of course. First of all they change into a *chrysalis* or *pupa*, which sometimes looks like a small barrel-shaped case attached to a leaf or stem. In this stage the insect does not feed, but inside the pupal case there are all kinds of physical changes going on as the body of the caterpillar is transformed into a butterfly. When the butterfly is ready to emerge, the skin of the pupa splits and the butterfly squeezes out. It then rests for an hour or two until the wings have dried and hardened.

All this takes between two and four weeks on

WHAT'S THE DIFFERENCE BETWEEN A BUTTERFLY AND A MOTH?

■ Most butterflies rest with their wings closed in an upright position. Moths close their wings flat over their back.

■ The antennae of butterflies are club-shaped at the tip. Most moths don't have club-shaped antennae.

■ Butterflies come out during the day. Moths tend to come out mainly at night.

average, depending on whether it's cool or warm weather. But there are some species which hibernate in the chrysalis – the green hairstreak and the speckled wood, for instance – and the change from caterpillar to butterfly can take up to nine months.

What's the biggest moth in the world?

In his new butterfly house at Windsor Safari Park, Terry has some atlas moths, which are candidates for being the largest moths in the world. Says Terry, "It all depends on whether you mean large in terms of surface area. In that case, the largest moth is probably the Hercules moth of Australia and Papua New Guinea. But if you mean large in terms of its wing span, then these giant atlas moths can be as much as 280 mm wide. They're tawny rather than brightly coloured, but the patterns on the wings are quite beautiful."

By the way, none of Terry's moths and butterflies are taken from the wild. They're all bred on butterfly farms and ranches in their native country. The law in some of these countries is to introduce ten per cent of the bred stock back into the wild every year. None of Terry's butterflies are listed as endangered species.

PLANTING FOR BUTTERFLIES

A garden planted with masses of flowers looks lovely, but a garden with flowers *and* butterflies is even more spectacular. Look at a buddleia bush, for instance, on a hot summer's day when there are lots of small tortoiseshell butterflies around. The movement of the butterflies' wings makes the plant seem alive with colour.

In general, butterflies go for flowers that are sweet-smelling and colourful, and have single rather than double blooms. But not all colours will do. Butterflies like certain colours and not others. Brimstones are attracted to yellow primroses, and in fact they are the chief pollinator of the primrose. The brimstones, too, are yellow, but that's probably just a coincidence.

White flowers are good. Candytuft will attract lesser peacocks, and arabis will bring in orange tips to feed on the nectar of the flowers and also to lay their eggs in the seed pods.

Purple is a very popular colour. Aubretia attracts small tortoiseshells and brimstones too, and the caterpillars of the green-veined white butterfly feed on its leaves. Two more purple flowers are

---

DO-IT-YOURSELF NECTAR

Here's a good idea if you don't have any flowers in your garden, or if you don't have a garden at all. Why not turn your bird table, or even your window box, into a "butterfly table", during the summer?

You can make your own "nectar" to attract butterflies by mixing together:

Half a teaspoon of honey
Half a teaspoon of caster sugar
A pinch of salt
Half a pint of water

Keep to the recipe and don't be tempted to make it any stronger. The honey makes a good feed for butterflies, and the smell helps to attract them. Once you've made the solution, pour a little into a saucer, and put cotton wool in the middle for the butterflies to land on. Or tie bits of cotton wool on thread, dip them in the solution and hang them from your bird table. It's important to keep the nectar off the ground, so that it doesn't attract ants.

Another good butterfly food is apples. Crush them up, until they're good and messy, and put them out on your butterfly table. And if you let them ferment in a jar first, the butterflies will find them even more attractive.

---

honesty, which is popular with orange tips, and sweet-smelling lavender.

Other flowers to plant or sow are alyssum, catmint, goldenrod, Michaelmas daisy, sweet william, thrift, valerian and *Sedum spectabile*. And the stinging nettle, a weed which most people think is nothing but a nuisance, is also an important plant – not for the butterflies, but for the caterpillars. Red admiral, peacock and small tortoiseshell caterpillars all feed on nettles. So don't cut down *all* the stinging nettles – leave a corner of the garden wild!

Remember that butterflies don't only feed on the nectar of your flowers, they also offer a service in return. As they gather nectar, they also gather pollen which clings to their bodies. Then, as they go from flower to flower, they fertilise other plants, and that starts the growth of new seeds.

BUTTERFLY COLOUR CHART

If you want to know what colour flowers to plant in your garden, or if you simply want to find out which colours butterflies like best, try making a butterfly colour chart. Make it good and big (about 400 cms wide), colour it in, and put pieces of cotton wool dipped in nectar solution on the individual colours.

You'll soon find out which colours are the most popular. But you'll also discover that different butterflies may prefer different colours: the small tortoiseshell, for instance, likes purple best, then pink, then white.

Note the landings of the individual species in the horizontal column, and at the end of the day mark down the totals in the vertical columns. When we tried it, purple came out tops.

PURPLE	GREEN	PINK	WHITE	RED	YELLOW	BLUE
TOTAL	TOTAL	TOTAL	TOTAL	TOTAL	TOTAL	TOTAL

Dear Ron, what is the most poisonous spider in the world? what colour is it what dose it eat? dose it Sting? dose it hurt people?.

What is the most poisonous spider in the world?

"Not more fan mail!" said Ron, wiping a tired pedipalp across his prosoma. He glanced quickly round the office to see how his mail compared with the bundles for Chris, Terry and Nick. His pile was definitely bigger, he thought to himself smugly. Actually it was pretty difficult for him to look round the office anyway, since his knees kept getting in the way of what his eight eyes could see.

Ron opened the first letter and began to read. "'What's the largest spider in the world?' The Guyanan bird-eating spider. 'What's the smallest spider in the world?' The pale yellow midget spider. Always the same old questions," thought Ron. "Oh for a task to stretch my intellect."

" 'What's the most poisonous spider in the world?' Not again," said Ron crossly. "The funnel-web, of course. Hang on a minute," he thought, "maybe it's the black widow." Or what about that massive South American cousin of his, *Phoneutria*? He could dish out the neurotoxins like nobody's business. Ron was getting confused and decided a break was called for. He walked round to Chris and Nick and sat himself down on their typewriter.

"Need any assistance, guys?" said Ron. Only a spider as sensitive as Ron could have picked up their unspoken cry for help. They looked at him with thanks, even adoration. Still, he was used to that.

"The thing is, Ron," said Chris, "we've got this letter with this really difficult question and we don't know what the answer is."

"The question is: 'What's the most dangerous animal in the world?' " said Nick. "Anything you can do to help, Ron? We'd be terribly grateful."

Ron's mind raced back to the last letter he'd read. "Bound to be a spider," he said. "You carry on with your research, if you want, but I'll find the

answer for you. See you in the studio later on for the show."

As Ron made his way through the endless corridors of BBC Bristol, he scratched his chest worriedly – that's where his extremely large brain was located. "The most dangerous animal in the world? It's all very well making these promises, but where do I start looking? I'll just have to do some in-depth research." As he happened to be walking through Reception at the time, Ron decided to start his in-depth research with the commissionaire.

· "Hey, Fred," he said, "what's the most dangerous animal in the world?"

Fred was obviously overwhelmed at being spoken to by the great tarantula, and it took him a few seconds to answer. "Tiger," he said, "or crocodile, maybe?"

Ron made a mental note. He hadn't thought of those.

"What do you think, Barbara?" he said, turning to the receptionist. Barbara was busy and seemed strangely unawed by Ron's presence. Ron clam-

bered on to the desk and repeated his question.

"Rattlesnakes, I'd say," said the receptionist. "Or maybe sharks?"

"Gosh," thought Ron, "I hadn't thought of *any* of those, and nobody's mentioned tarantulas yet!"

"Why not try the library?" asked Barbara.

"I don't need reference books to answer a simple question," retorted Ron, heading for the library as fast as his eight legs could carry him.

"How about piranha fish?" said Sue, the librarian.

"Good idea," said Ron.

"We've got some film you can use on the programme. I'll look it out for you."

Ron looked at the film in the cutting room, and

was definitely not impressed. They looked rather sweet fish and not very dangerous at all. "Didn't you hear of that bus that drove into the River Amazon in 1976, and all thirty-one people on board were eaten by piranhas?" asked Sue. Ron's heart started to pump fast and he had to breathe extra carefully through the four lungs sticking out of his tummy. The one thing he didn't want now was even more suggestions from the two film editors.

"I reckon the most dangerous animal to man is the hippo," said Della.

"That's only in wetland Africa," said Angie. "In dryland Africa, the Cape buffalo kills more people than any other animal."

"Stop, stop!" cried Ron. "Suggestions I've got. What I need now is facts!"

Half an hour later, Ron had bribed himself into the computer room with a few generously distributed autographs. He quickly typed in the password to get into *The Really Wild Show* database, then he crossed his spinnerets and started checking his list of animals.

RATTLESNAKES: PROBABLY 16–20 DEATHS A YEAR.
TARANTULAS: OF 26 SPECIES, ONLY 12 DANGEROUS TO MAN. PRODUCES ONLY LOW-GRADE NEUROTOXIN VENOM, NORMALLY HARMLESS.

"How disappointing," thought Ron. "I mustn't tell anybody about that. No one will take me seriously any more."

SHARKS: PROBABLY 100 HUMAN DEATHS A YEAR.
CROCODILES: ESTUARINE CROCS KILL 2,000 PEOPLE A YEAR WORLDWIDE.

million people in the world die of malaria. In fact the malaria mosquito is probably responsible for almost half of all human deaths, not counting wars and accidents. That's about 27,000 million people!"

Ron had to endure a flood of insults from Blondy as they tried to sneak out of the studio without being seen. "Those mosquitoes make me look about as dangerous as a marshmallow," he said.

"Charming!" thought Ron. "You try to help your friends and this is what you get. There's just no gratitude!"

Top: Nick and a black rat in the studio
Bottom: A malaria mosquito – full of blood!

"Now we're getting somewhere," thought Ron. "But how am I going to be able to get the most dangerous animal in the world to the studio in an hour's time?"

Ron confided his problem to Vicky, the make-up artist who, a short while later, was giving him a quick wash and blow-dry.

"What about your blonde friend?" suggested Vicky. "You know, the great big, dangerous one."

"You mean *Theraphosa Leblondi*? Brilliant idea. I mean, just what I was going to suggest."

Blondy was a particularly huge Guyanan bird-eating spider. And he was pretty nasty with it.

A quick phone call and half an hour later, Ron strolled into the studio arm in arm with his giant spider friend, to be met with hoots of scorn from the studio audience. "The most dangerous animal in the world!" they laughed. "That's nothing compared to what Nick Davies has got."

"These are black rats," said Nick. "They may look pretty harmless, but back in the fourteenth century they were responsible for spreading the Great Plague throughout Europe. Millions of people died of the plague. In just four years, one-third of the entire population of Europe was killed. The rats spread the plague, but the animals which actually caused the disease were the creatures on them. And they were fleas – rat fleas. When the fleas bit people to feed on their blood, they spread the bubonic plague."

Ron was abashed, but his humiliation was not over yet, because now it was Chris's turn to introduce his animal.

"But even the rat flea isn't the most dangerous animal in the world to man. That title must go to another insect, the malaria mosquito. Each year, a

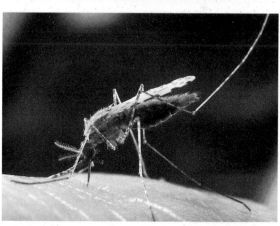

PETS

You may have foreign visitors in your home and not even know it! Perhaps you have a gerbil from Africa, an Australian budgie or even a goldfish from China. All of these animals, and many more, have become common pets. Sometimes they behave in ways that would be natural for them in the wild but make us wonder what they are doing. Here are some of your questions about pets answered.

Why does my dog howl when the EastEnders theme tune is on the telly?

In the wild, dogs howl to call each other together to form a pack but most pet dogs live alone and don't need to do this. Sometimes a dog will hear a note or tone that it mistakes for another dog howling; it may be on the television or a musical instrument in the home. It then calls back to answer the pack. So howling dogs aren't just good singers – they are actually trying to organise a hunting expedition.

WARNING

PETS CAN SERIOUSLY

IMPROVE

YOUR HEALTH!

Believe it or not, pets are good for you. They can help some people to live longer, healthier lives, which may explain the stories about all those little old ladies with cats! Dogs and cats are especially good for you. Stroking a cat is very relaxing and can lower blood pressure which reduces the risk of stress and heart attacks; and walking the dog is healthy exercise. In America you can even buy videos of tropical fish, complete with relaxing bubble noises, to make your television look like a fish tank!

I would like to know if dogs see in black and white or in colour.

For a long time it was thought that dogs only saw in black and white, but it's now believed that they can see some colours. They can't tell the difference between red and green but they can see blues fairly well and are good at distinguishing shapes.

What is the most popular childrens pet

· TOP · OF · THE ·
PETS

No 1 Dogs	27% of UK households
Cats	21%
Fish	14%
Birds	9%
Hamsters, Gerbils and Rabbits	6%

Please could you tell me what the biggest and smallest dog in the world is thank you

The biggest dog in the world in weight is the St Bernard which can weigh as much as 140 kg. That's twice as heavy as an average man, and 200 times heavier than the world's smallest dog, the chihuahua, which weighs in at just 680 grammes.

Dear Really Wild Show,

I would like to know what cat is the heaviest in the world and what is its name?

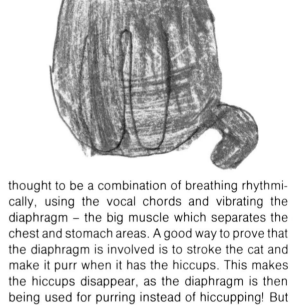

The heaviest cat in the world is no longer alive but his name was 'Himmy' and he weighed in at 20.7 kg. That's almost as heavy as ten normal cats.

Why do cats purr and how do they do it

Cats purr for many reasons, but how they do it is a bit of a mystery. A purr can have several different meanings. Kittens purr when they are suckling to tell their mother that they are happy and getting plenty of milk, and she purrs back to reassure them. But a purr doesn't always mean happiness – cats also purr in times of distress and pain.

We don't know exactly how cats purr but it is thought to be a combination of breathing rhythmically, using the vocal chords and vibrating the diaphragm – the big muscle which separates the chest and stomach areas. A good way to prove that the diaphragm is involved is to stroke the cat and make it purr when it has the hiccups. This makes the hiccups disappear, as the diaphragm is then being used for purring instead of hiccupping! But have you ever seen a cat with the hiccups?!

my Favourite Animal IS a rabbit here is a picture OF one

From kirstie

Why does my cat need to sleep for so long every day?

In the wild, cats are only active at dawn and dusk. They spend the rest of the time lazing about and sleeping. They hunt and eat and then rest. Cats spend up to 16 hours of a 24-hour day asleep. That means if your cat is 6 years old it's only actually been awake for 2 years of its life!

Why does my cat have static electricity in his fur that sometimes gives me a shock when I stroke him?

Electric cats is a shocking phenomenon! Cats can become charged up with extra energy because they have very smooth fur which is a good insulator and can keep hold of heat or, in this case, electricity. Cats tend to collect electric charges in their fur when they roll or walk on nylon carpets and these can shoot into your fingers as a shock when you stroke them. Believe it or not, some cats have been seen to spark in the dark!

> **Cats** can detect earthquakes because they are very sensitive to tremors and changes in the earth.

Can you tell the age of a tortoise by its shell?

Yes and no is the answer to this question! Tortoises' shells are made up of plates, and each year, until the tortoise reaches its maximum size, it adds another growth ring, in much the same way as trees do. But it's not that easy to tell a tortoise's age! Baby tortoises can hatch with as many as forty rings already on their shells, and old tortoises may not have grown any new rings for years.

> **Tortoises** have jelly in their stomachs! Their digestive juices form a jelly which doesn't melt until they are warm enough to eat.

why do cats Rub their faces against humans and furniture alike? surely they can't love them both the same!

Cats rub themselves on people and furniture for a very good reason and it's not just to get a free stroke! It's all to do with swopping smells. When a cat rubs itself on you, it leaves behind a scent from the glands by its mouth and on its brow; but with its back end it takes away some of *your* smell, which it tastes later when it washes. When they rub against furniture they leave their smell to mark out their territory and have a quick check for other smells. So if you've got a cat, you're a marked person in a marked house!

Why does the Manx cat have no tail?

There are all sorts of tales about Manx cats' tails! Some stories say that sailors brought them back from Japan and others that they were the last animals into Noah's ark and that he slammed the door on their tails. The truth is that at some stage, a freak cat without a tail must have been born on the Isle of Man. It passed this tail-less characteristic on to the next generation and, as time went on, cats without tails became more and more common. Proper Manx cats have no signs of even the tiniest tails and have a hollow at the end of their back bones. Some are born with little tails and they are known as 'Stumpies'.

Why do hamsters die young?

It's all to do with how fast their hearts beat. Every mammal's heart beats about 800 million times before it dies. Hamsters' hearts beat very fast, and they have "used up" all their heart beats in about four years. Elephants' hearts on the other hand, beat quite slowly, and they can live for more than fifty years.

  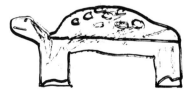

Why do a mouse's teeth never wear out?

The teeth of rodents like mice are continually growing and that's why they never wear out. The more a mouse gnaws and nibbles, the sharper its teeth get. In fact, mice have got to keep eating to keep up with the growth of their teeth. It's not unknown for the teeth of sick or old mice to grow so long that they pass through the jaws, stopping them from opening their mouths.

How fast can a gerbil eat?

When a gerbil is furiously putting food into its mouth it isn't actually eating it – it's filling up its pouches. Gerbils don't eat very fast but they do fill up their mouths at great speed. They do this so that they can take the food away and store it to eat later on. A record-sized stack of food, measuring one metre in height and three metres in length, has been found outside a gerbil's burrow.

Old Age Pets – O A P S

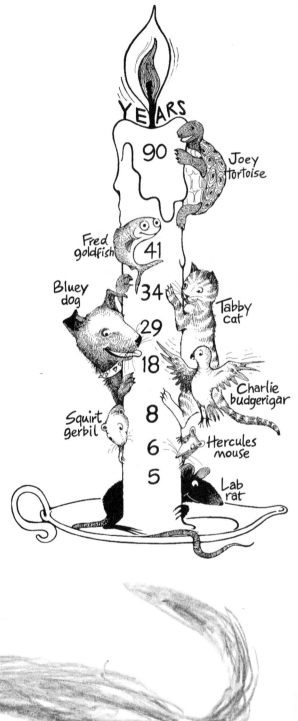

YEARS

90 — Joey Tortoise
41 — Fred goldfish
34 — Tabby cat
29 — Bluey dog
18
8 — Charlie budgerigar
Squirt gerbil
6 — Hercules mouse
5 — Lab rat

Why do rabbits have big ears?

Big ears are very good for gathering sound but they can also be used to control how hot the animal gets. English Lopp rabbits have the biggest ears, but they are very floppy. The black-tailed jack rabbit probably has the biggest useful ears. They have a large area of skin with lots of veins so that, if the animal gets too hot, extra blood can be made to flow close to the skin surface to cool the animal down.

How did animals get invented

NICK DAVIES EXPLAINS:

Inventing something means coming up with an idea for a new sort of object . . . like a telephone or a car . . . and then, getting on and making it.

Animals aren't just objects, so they can't be invented like a new sort of machine. All animals and plants have come into being because of *evolution*, happening over millions of years.

The first person to understand how evolution worked was Charles Darwin. He wrote his ideas in 1859 in a famous book called *On the Origin of Species.*

Scientists today don't know exactly how it works in detail, but Darwin's theory is still thought to be true.

Darwin's theory says that a species – that's a kind of animal – doesn't stay the same for ever. One species can change, or *evolve*, into another. So, after many millions of years, lots of different species of animals appear . . .

Here's an example of how one species can turn into another . . .

Suppose there's a species of bird that eats seeds. Some birds have bigger beaks than others, but most of the time that doesn't matter and all the birds do as well as each other.

Then, there's a drought. All the plants die and

THE EVOLUTION OF THE HORSE

The Horse today
Equus

Mesohippus
lived about
30 million
years ago

Hyracotherium
lived about 60 million
years ago

and who did invented them.

the small seeds are eaten up. Only big seeds are left. Only the birds with the big beaks can eat them, so all the birds with small beaks starve to death. The species has changed to one where all the beaks are big.

That's almost exactly what happened to the Galapagos ground finch in the drought of 1977. Only big-beaked birds survived, so now the species is different from its pre-1977 form.

Of course change doesn't have to be that sudden. Take a leaf-eating animal such as the giraffe. If trees got taller over a long time, then with each generation of leaf-eaters, animals with longer legs would get more food and have more babies. So over many generations the species would be made up of more animals with longer and longer legs.

All this is really to say that if anything "invented" animals then it was evolution. So that's the "how" and the "who", but what about the "when"? When were animals invented?

Here's a potted history of life on earth.

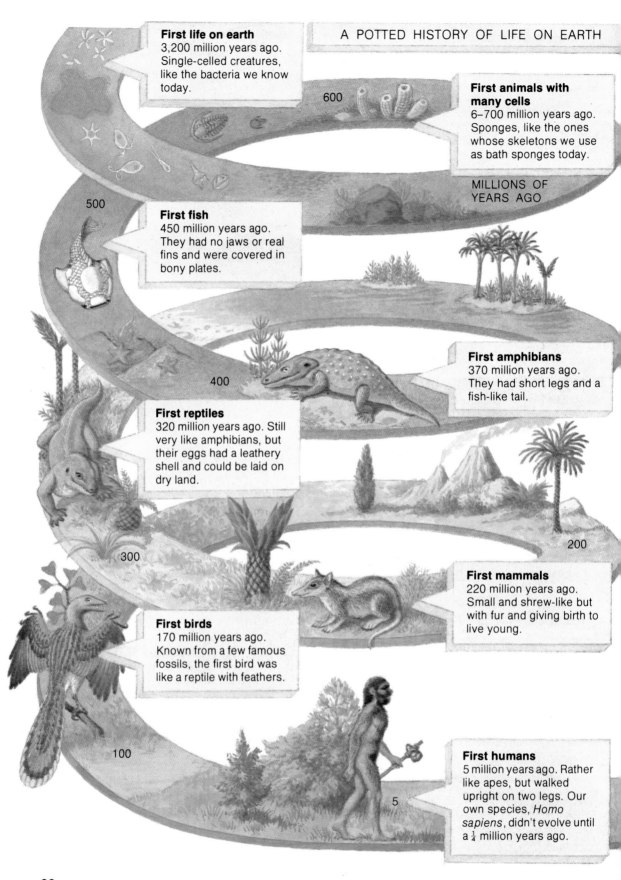

First life on earth
3,200 million years ago.
Single-celled creatures,
like the bacteria we know
today.

600

**First animals with
many cells**
6–700 million years ago.
Sponges, like the ones
whose skeletons we use
as bath sponges today.

MILLIONS OF
YEARS AGO

500

First fish
450 million years ago.
They had no jaws or real
fins and were covered in
bony plates.

First amphibians
370 million years ago.
They had short legs and a
fish-like tail.

400

First reptiles
320 million years ago. Still
very like amphibians, but
their eggs had a leathery
shell and could be laid on
dry land.

200

300

First mammals
220 million years ago.
Small and shrew-like but
with fur and giving birth to
live young.

First birds
170 million years ago.
Known from a few famous
fossils, the first bird was
like a reptile with feathers.

100

First humans
5 million years ago. Rather
like apes, but walked
upright on two legs. Our
own species, *Homo
sapiens*, didn't evolve until
a $\frac{1}{4}$ million years ago.

5

36

Dear Ron...

How long are your legs and how much do you weigh?

This is a good opportunity for Ron to parade his vital statistics! His legs are actually different

lengths. At first glance it looks as if he has 10 legs, but the top pair are pedipalps which are used rather like hands. Each of his first and fourth pairs of legs measures 700 mm, and each of his second and third pairs measures 550 mm. Ron weighs in at 20 g, about the same weight as a £1 coin.

What is the largest and most fierce tarantula?

Tarantulas are some of the biggest spiders in the world. The largest tarantula doesn't have a common name but its Latin name is *Theraphosa leblondi* and it comes from South America, just like Ron. One male of this type grew to have a leg span of 254 mm – that's nearly as long as this page!

What about fierce tarantulas? Well, big tarantulas can make themselves look very fierce by rearing up the front of their bodies and this scares away other animals. Despite looking fierce, most tarantulas are not very dangerous. The small poisonous spiders, such as black widows, are the ones to worry about!

What do tarantulas eat?

Tarantulas are meat-eaters and hunt their food. They eat anything that moves and is small enough for them to catch, mainly insects. Ron's favourite foods are locusts and crickets. He sometimes eats as many as six a week. Wild tarantulas have been known to eat bigger meals like small lizards, snakes and even baby birds.

Are there any animals that can kill tarantulas?

Tarantulas don't have very many enemies because they can scare most of them away by rearing up to look big. They can also flick their bristles into the faces of their enemies, like little darts. These bristles cause irritation, itching and even sneezing. While all this is going on, the tarantula can escape.

There is only one animal that the tarantula doesn't scare – the hunting wasp. Hunting wasps are very quick and can sting and paralyse tarantulas.

Where does the name 'tarantula' come from?

The name tarantula is said to have originated in the town of Taranto in Italy, where they had a strange idea that tarantula bites caused a disease called 'tarantism'. The only known cure was to perform a feverish dance – the tarantella – to sweat out the poison.

The Commonest Bird in Britain

This is probably one of the questions Chris gets asked most of all on *The Really Wild Show*. The trouble is, there's no certain answer – or rather the answer changes depending on the time of year, which part of the country you live in, and whether you live in the town or in the country.

The answer also depends on lots of dedicated bird-watchers counting birds all over the country and sending in their figures for the annual Common Birds Census.

In winter, the starling is usually the most common bird in Britain. That's because their numbers increase with the arrival of starlings from Scandinavia, migrating to Britain for the winter. The house sparrow must also be very near the top of the list. They are very common in towns, of course, but by contrast are very scarce in parts of Britain not inhabited by man. The chaffinch is another bird whose numbers increase in winter, with large numbers of birds migrating to Britain from the Netherlands. Blackbirds are very common. Although they used to live purely in woodlands, they have now adapted to living and breeding on farmland and in gardens and parks. Woodpigeons deserve a place in the Top Five, helped by their very long breeding season, which lasts from April to October.

Starling

Wren

The wren illustrates just how difficult it is to decide which is the commonest bird in Britain. Between 1964 and 1974, after a series of mild winters, the population of the wren increased tenfold; and at the end of this period there were an estimated 10 million pairs. But many birds died during the bad winter of 1978, and the number of wrens fell dramatically. But if this winter is mild, the wren may once again be "top of the pops".

Chaffinch

The Biggest Leaf in the World

The giant Amazonian water lily has the largest leaves of any plant in the world. They're 2 metres across and can support the weight of a 6-year-old child. Emily Hayward and Nick saw these leafy giants growing at Kew Gardens in London.

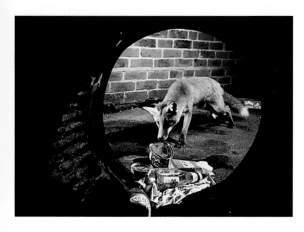

· FOX AND DUSTBIN ·
1st prize. Urban wildlife 1985

Chris took this picture in the driveway of his own house. He took the bottom out of the dustbin and placed his lights and camera, which was operated by an infra-red remote-control, inside. It took many nights to get the wild fox used to the set-up, but eventually Chris got this super shot.

TERRY: Chris Packham isn't just a pretty face! He isn't just an extraordinary hair-do on top of Superman's body. He isn't just a writer, actor, poet, film cameraman, television presenter, expert ornithologist, and all-round good egg ... How am I doing so far, Chris?

CHRIS: You're doing all right, Tel. Just don't forget about the outrageous dress-sense, and the Aston Martin.

TERRY: Sorry. Yes, Chris is all those things and, as if that wasn't enough, he's an international wildlife stills photographer ...

WILDLIFE PHOTOGRAPHER OF THE YEAR

CHRIS: And he's climbed the tallest tree in Britain, Tel.

TERRY: Yes, he's done that too.

CHRIS: Sixty metres high, it was.

TERRY: Sixty metres high and still growing. And here are the photographs which have won him awards three years in a row. How did I do, Chris?

CHRIS: Not bad, Terry. Here's your fiver.

· DEAD FISH ·
1st prize. Composition and Form 1986

Chris acquired the subject of this winning picture on a three-week tour of the Scottish Highlands and Islands, and kept it with him in the car, despite the protests of the three friends he was travelling with. Back home in Southampton, he sprayed the fish very slightly with gold paint to show up the texture of the scales and enhance the light. He also sprayed the concrete backdrop, and lit the fish with gold reflectors to give the effect he wanted.

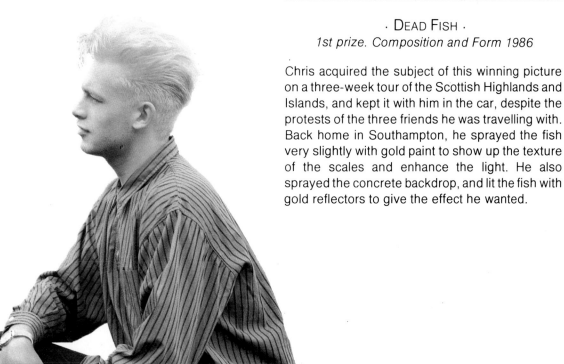

· GULL ON ICE ·
2nd prize. Composition and Form 1986

Chris noticed the subject of this picture on an iced-over lake near his home. A group of black-headed gulls were roosting on the ice and, after a while, one of them broke away and landed on its own. Chris took only one photograph before the bird flew away.

· STAG BEETLE ·
1st prize. Composition and Form 1987

One of the four books Chris is currently writing is about woodlands and he admits to being fascinated by stag beetles, one of his favourite woodland animals. But he came across this one in a churchyard in which a hearse was parked. Chris put the stag beetle on the highly reflective bonnet and got this remarkable, rather bizarre shot.

Animals in Danger

Can you imagine a time in Britain when packs of wolves and wild boar wandered the forests and large brown bears lay sleepily in caves? Several hundred years ago these animals really did live in Britain, but they are now all extinct. Sadly other animals are following their tracks and every year a few more plants and animals disappear never to be seen again. Strangely, it's the most intelligent but most thoughtless animal that is causing most of the problems – man. Nature is very carefully balanced and if this balance is disturbed, animals can disap-

pear alarmingly fast. Since the year 1900, for instance, 53 birds and 68 mammals worldwide have been wiped out. Fortunately, it is not too late for most animals and the future lies in understanding what is going wrong and putting it right. Your *Really Wild Show* letters show that you do care and want to know more, so hopefully you will be able to help save some animals for the future.

I'm sorry but I'm dead against rare animals being killed for skin or money

WILD WORRIES

ANIMAL SPECIES IN DANGER TODAY

The dodo was a huge bird rather like a pigeon that lived on the island of Mauritius in the Indian Ocean. It couldn't fly, but that didn't matter until man arrived and began to hunt it. Because it couldn't fly away, it was an easy target for the hunters and its numbers soon began to fall. The dodo died out completely in the seventeenth century, largely because sailors on the way to the Far East killed it for food.

Why are big animals in more danger than small animals?

Both large and small animals are in danger, but often it's the large ones, like rhinos and whales, that we notice most. Big animals are especially in danger when their numbers become very low, because it takes a long time for them to grow and breed again. Small animals like flies can have lots of young in no time at all; but animals like whales may take seven years to grow big enough to breed and then another year to have a single baby.

I am worried that soon there re going to be no whales left in the world. Do some whales die because of pollution? or by hunting?

There are still quite a few whales left in the world but four species are in trouble and have been classified as *endangered*.

Bowhead whale – 7300 left
Right whale – 2000 left
Blue whale – 10 000 left
Humpback whale – 11 000 left

(It is very difficult to count whales so these figures are only estimates.) Hunting has been the major reason for the fall in the numbers of whales. Nowadays not much hunting is allowed and commercial whaling is due to stop completely in 1988. Today's problems were caused by hunters earlier on in the last century who killed vast numbers of whales without thinking about the effect that this might have. Blue whales were especially popular since they are so enormous; and in the 1860s, so many were killed in the North Atlantic that hunters had to find other places to go. As the big whales started to disappear, the hunters started on the smaller ones – bowheads were caught for oil and right whales were popular because, unlike other whales, they floated to the surface when dead.

Pollution isn't a serious problem for whales, although oil, chemicals and old netting can block the filters that they use to collect the small organisms they feed on. Another unexpected sort of pollution is that of noise, such as drills and propellers. This can make it difficult for whales to call to each other over the thousands of miles of oceans and thus meet up.

DON'T KILL THE WHALE

I am especially worried about the cheetah because of it's fantastic shiny black spotted yellow coat

from Thomas (age 6)

I am worried that the cheetah may become extinct.

Hopefully, the cheetah will never become extinct. At the moment it is said to be *vulnerable*, which means that it could move into the most endangered group of animals. Although cheetah numbers are low in Asia and even worse in the Middle East, there are still about 25 000 in Africa.

Some years ago cheetahs were killed for their beautiful coats. Thousands and thousands of animals were sacrificed for the sake of fashion. Even today some spotted cats are killed – a strange thing to do when the skins look much better on cheetahs themselves.

Today the biggest problem for cheetahs is man taking over their living and hunting areas. When this happens, the cheetahs are restricted to a small area and this means that there are fewer animals for them to hunt. Cheetahs are also then more likely to come into contact with man and domestic animals, and many are shot for killing cattle. Another new problem for cheetahs is disturbance from tourists in national parks. Tourists follow the cheetahs in landrovers. This disturbs them when they are hunting, and frightens away their prey.

RARE ANIMALS
· *on our doorstep* ·

What was the last animal to become extinct in England?

The last animal to become extinct in England was an insect – the large blue butterfly – and it is thought to have disappeared in 1979. It lived on chalk downland and had a very specialised life style. The caterpillars were protected and fed by an ant and in return they provided the ants with honey from a gland on their bodies. As the special chalk downland disappeared, so did the butterflies. But there is good news – a very similar species, from Switzerland, has been introduced and seems to be doing well.

Above: Large blue butterfly
Left: Greater horseshoe bat

British vanishing species

Animals and plants are becoming rare on our own doorsteps. The main reason is that the places they live in are being destroyed.

We must try and save the . . .
Dartford warbler
Red-backed shrike
Avocet
Swallowtail butterfly
Great crested newt
Smooth snake
Dormouse
Ghost orchid
Military orchid
Mouse-eared bat (only one male left in Britain)
Horseshoe bat

BEING INVOLVED WITH RARE ANIMALS

If you want to know more about rare animals you can write to the following addresses. Don't forget to enclose a stamped addressed envelope.

Young Peoples Trust for Endangered Species

19 Quarry Street
Guildford
Surrey
GU1 3EH

World Wildlife Fund

Panda House
11–13 Ockford Road
Godalming
Surrey
GU7 1QU

THE RAREST ANIMAL IN THE WORLD

The most difficult question to answer is:

What is the rarest animal in the whole wide world?

There are many animals that are very rare and it is very difficult to choose one. But if you look at page 58, you will see an animal that is certainly one of the rarest.

DINOSAUR FACTS

What was the longest dinosaur?
Diplodocus was the longest – up to 28 metres long. Most of this was neck and tail – in fact, its tail alone measured 14 metres!

What was the heaviest dinosaur?
Brachiosaurus weighed in at 80 tonnes – about the same as nine fully grown elephants. But there may have been individuals that weighed as much as 100 tonnes. Despite its size it was a gentle, plant-eating animal.

What was the smallest dinosaur?
Compsognathus was no bigger than a chicken – about 0.65 metres long. It probably hunted insects and small mammals, and was a very efficient killer because, although it was tiny, it had sharp teeth and claws. Scientists think it might have looked rather like a bird, but without feathers or wings.

What was the fiercest dinosaur?
Tyrannosaurus rex – the largest carnivore ever known. It had long, serrated teeth for tearing flesh.

The name means "Tyrant King of the Lizards" and, reared up on its hind legs to a height of 5 metres, it must have been a terrible sight indeed. But although it was big and fierce, it wasn't very fast. Luckily for Tyrannosaurus rex, there were enough even slower dinosaurs around for it to catch. No one quite knows what its tiny front limbs were for. They couldn't have been used for feeding because they were too short to reach its mouth.

What was the stupidest dinosaur?

Probably Stegosaurus. Although weighing about 2 tonnes, its brain was tiny – only about the size of a walnut. It used to be thought that this dinosaur had a second brain near its tail to give it a bit of a hand. Everyone knows Stegosaurus as the dinosaur with the big plates down his back and four spikes on the end of its tail. Scientists now think that the plates were used to control the animal's body temperature.

What was the fastest dinosaur?

Probably Hypsilophodon – a small, docile, grass-eating dinosaur, whose only defence against attack was to use its speed to run away. It was light, weighing about 65 kg, and only 1.5 metres long.

Top: Diplodocus. Bottom left: Compsognathus. Bottom right: Stegosaurus. (All drawn to scale.)

Why did dinosaurs die out?

Dinosaurs ruled the earth for about 135 million years, while our ancestors were still only shrew-like creatures. There were hundreds of types of dinosaurs. Yet large or small, all these reptiles died out over a very short period of time – a blinking of the eye by geological standards. Why did they become extinct? There have been all sorts of theories, from epidemics and a world-wide temp-erature drop, to mammals eating all the dinosaurs' eggs.

Death Star

But the newest theory is all to do with space, and a star which nobody has ever seen – a wandering "death star" that visits our solar system every 26 million years. Sounds ridiculous? Well, the theory is not as far-fetched as you might think. Let's have a look at the evidence.

Ever since life first appeared on earth, there have been major disasters, when huge numbers of animals became extinct. For instance, if we go back about 247 million years – long before dinosaurs existed – half the known animals died out. In our box you'll see which creatures were wiped out at various times. Although not everyone agrees over the exact dates, many researchers think there is sufficient evidence to suggest that, roughly every 26 million years or so, a major disas-ter has struck the earth.

What exactly were these disasters?

Scientists interested in the problem have turned their attention to outer space – to the *Oort Cloud*, a cloud of meteorites orbiting the sun in deep space. If that cloud is disturbed, our solar system would be bombarded by showers of meteorites, some of which could hit our planet. Vast dust clouds would be raised, plunging the earth into darkness and wiping out huge numbers of plants and animals.

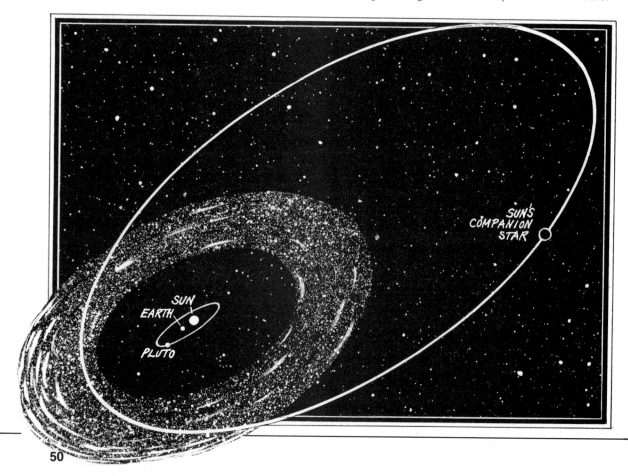

DEATH STAR

How could the cloud be disturbed in the first place?

Research teams led by two British physicists say it could be caused by a wandering star, called Nemesis, that has never been seen. Nemesis may be a companion star of the sun, with an orbit lasting 26 million years, unlike our one-year orbit. When Nemesis comes round our side of the sun, it passes the Oort Cloud, disturbing the meteorites and causing widespread death and destruction.

So what about the future?

There's no need for us to worry too much. If it exists at all, Nemesis isn't due for another 15 million years. By that time, scientists may well have found a way to deflect it away from us. At last, one of the great mysteries of science may have an explanation: "Dinosaurs were made extinct by a death star." Of course, it's only a theory – but do you have a better one . . .?

ANIMAL EXTINCTIONS	
Millions of years ago	**Extinctions**
247	Rostrococnes (clam-like creatures, but without the hinges) and most of the trilobites (forerunners of the modern horseshoe crab).
220–208	Condononts (jellyfish-like animals) and many reptiles.
194	Huge numbers of marine animals.
163	Primitive reptiles and amphibians that had dominated the land. (These were replaced by the early dinosaurs.)
144	Dinoflagellates (simple sea-living organisms).
120	Cephalopods (squid-like sea creatures).
65	The most dramatic extinction of all – dinosaurs and many other life forms.
38	Coccoliths (tiny marine organisms).
11	Foraminiferans (single-celled sea animals).

I WANT TO MEET A
KOALA

I am seven years old and I would like to meer a koala.

my Koala from Craig age 7

Please may I see a Live KOaLa-Bear infront of my very eyes

Love Stuart

I am 5 from Maxthew

Just look at these letters – just some of the hundreds to *The Really Wild Show*, all from children who want to meet a koala. Early on in the series, we selected a few children who'd written in to the programme about animals they wanted to meet – that's how Ron made his first appearance, on the hand of Marc Sheddon from Cardigan. Spiders, anacondas and pumas were difficult, but not impossible to arrange – but a koala! For a start, there aren't any koalas outside Australia, except in zoos in California.

So there was only one way out of the problem. We had to fly to Australia. British Airways kindly offered us help, but there was only space for one koala-lover. So we put all the names into the hat, and the lucky winner was 10-year-old Claire Swift from Wigan.

It was all done in a tremendous rush. I was in the studio in BBC Birmingham, and before the recording session ended, I had to be whisked off in a car to London Airport, leaving Terry and Chris to finish off the show. A quick hello to Claire at Terminal 1, and then we had a flight of twenty hours or so in which to get to know each other.

Claire told me that, in her spare time, she helps muck out and feed some of the animals at a zoo near her home in Wigan. "I've looked after wallabies and emus", she told me, "but I've always wanted to hold a koala – they look so cuddly". But would they really be cuddly, I thought to myself? After all, these are wild animals, not teddy bears. I hoped Claire wasn't going to be disappointed.

After landing in Sydney, Australia, Claire and I gave ourselves a day off to recover from the flight and do a whistle-stop tour of the sites. But early next morning, we drove to a park just outside the city where koalas are allowed to roam free. Here Claire had her first close-up view of the animal she'd travelled 11,000 miles across the world to see.

The koalas were all around us. Some were high up in the branches of the trees, some were dozing half-way up in the forks of branches, and some were right in front of us, fast asleep. Yes, they looked just like teddy bears. "I want to take one home," was the first thing Claire said.

We were allowed to stroke, but not to hold, a female koala with a baby riding on its back. As everybody knows, koalas are marsupials and the young are initially brought up in the mother's pouch where they suckle on one of the two nipples. But after seven months, young koalas travel on their mother's back, feeding on a mixed diet of milk and leaves. Claire and I discovered that koalas feel as soft and cuddly as they look. And Claire was surprised to discover they smelled minty – that's because of the eucalyptus leaves they eat.

But Claire soon realised that koalas are tough little animals too. Over 40 metres above her head, she could see koalas climbing up the most slender of branches which were whipping back and forth in the very strong winds. But there's no danger of them falling off. They have sharp claws on their hands and hind feet which lets them almost "bound" up vertical trunks. And on the koala she was stroking, Claire could see the "split" hand, with the first two fingers opposite the other three, so it can encircle a branch.

Claire went on to see emus, kangaroos, wallabies and wombats. Then, after only three days in Australia, still hardly able to believe what had happened, she was on her way home. A few weeks later, the film was shown on *The Really Wild Show* and Claire became quite a celebrity in her home town. Her final comment on koalas: "I think they're brilliant!"

Koala Facts

■ Koalas aren't bears.

■ Koalas are marsupials: they carry their young in a pouch.

■ Koalas eat leaves – mainly the leaves of certain gum or eucalyptus trees.

■ Koalas normally never drink – there is enough water in the leaves they eat.

■ Koalas can eat poison! Some eucalyptus leaves contain cyanide, but the koala has a specialised digestive system to cope with this and the strong-smelling eucalyptus oil.

■ Koalas sleep most of the day. They're nocturnal animals, moving about and feeding at night.

■ There used to be many koalas in Australia. But towards the end of the last century they were killed in large numbers for their skins. Nowadays they're totally protected, but even so large-scale forest clearances continue to deprive the koala of its food. This, together with disease, may mean that even today the koala is in danger. Only careful management by scientists will ensure its survival.

HAPPY BIRTHDAY, RON!

February 17th is Ron's official birthday. In the last series, Terry, Nick and Chris announced the coming of the great event at the end of the programme the week before. And, as you can see the birthday cards flooded in.

When the day came, half-way through the show, Chris wheeled on to the studio floor the most enormous birthday cake that Ron had ever seen. He was terribly pleased of course and didn't have the heart to tell Chris that he wasn't over-keen on icing, and could he have a few glazed locusts on top, please.

But surprise, surprise, it wasn't a real birthday cake at all, for Chris lifted off the top and inside were **hundreds of spiders.** Yes, it was all Ron's friends and relations, who'd come along to wish him a happy birthday.

Cameramen fainted, the floor manager turned green, in fact all the adults, quite predictably, made a dash for the door, as the spiders started crawling up and out of the cake. What a bunch of wimps! But the children in the audience weren't a bit fright-

ened, and they rushed forward to be introduced to a really interesting collection of arachnids.

There were pink-toed and orange-tipped tarantulas, there were cinnamon and gold tarantulas. In fact Ron, with his red knees, felt quite drab. He consoled himself by thinking that red was much more butch. But then suddenly Ron turned round and came prosoma to prosoma with the most beautiful female tarantula he'd ever seen. She was jet black with just a few bright red bristles on her large, curvaceous opisthosoma.

"Hey, amigo," said Ron in his heaviest Mexican accent, "whadd-ya tink od de show?"

"Ees-a not bad, leetle boy. But in Guatemala, we prefer real men!" and she headed off in the direction of Blondy. But Ron was too arrogant to feel offended.

There were trapdoor spiders, there were funnel web and purse web spiders, there were wolf spiders, hunting spiders and sun spiders. But Ron was most interested in meeting four of his relatives that live in Britain.

One of these is actually a tarantula! Yes, there is a British tarantula. It's *Atypus affinis*, the European purse web spider. It lives in a silk tube shaped like a sock through which it sticks its fangs to catch prey, dragging the bodies inside and then carefully mending the tear. "But don't worry," said Ron, "*Atypus* is only 8 mm long."

Next Ron was introduced to Britain's biggest spider, Dolomedes – the raft spider. "I'm a fishing spider," said Dol. "I live in the Fens in Norfolk, but we've been doing quite badly lately. But there are a lot of kind people who've been digging us special pits where it stays nice and wet all the year round, so there's a few more of us around now."

Ron was really impressed by Dolomedes. His body alone measured 22 mm, and that didn't include his enormous legs.

The hero of the previous week's programme was loudly applauded. He'd won the title of "The Fastest Spider In The World" and was still revelling in his glory. He was British as well – one of the *Tegenaria* – and he was boasting that he might even be the biggest, as well as the fastest, British spider, if you measured his leg span.

Ron was pleasantly surprised to meet yet another British spider – even if he was only a rather distant relative – who was also a world record holder. This was the slender and very shy harvestman. According to *The Really Wild Show* computer, he had the longest legs of any animal in the world, relative to his body size.

But this was Ron's day. By tarantula standards, he was still a youngster on this, his seventh, birthday. Tarantulas are the longest-lived of all spiders and females can live to be more than twenty. One female tarantula, collected in Mexico, was thought to have hatched in 1923 and she lived until 1951, thus reaching the ripe old age of twenty-eight.

Since there were a hundred different species of spider at his party, Ron worked out that he'd need another thirty birthdays before he'd be able to invite all the different spiders in the world. "After all," said Ron, "I do have 30,000 different species of spider as my relatives!"

Above: Dolomedes – the raft spider

THE RAREST BIRD IN BRITAIN

I saw my first red-backed shrike in 1976. It was a day I shall never forget. It was blazing hot and I was walking up a heathland track in the New Forest, the gravel path burning so brightly it made me squint, and the bees buzzing madly. Then, on the side of the path, in a piece of bramble under a holly bush, I saw a small bird. I looked through my cheapo' binoculars and KAA POWW! – I fell stupidly for a lovely little pastel-coloured bird which flew off without a trace.

I had recognised him instantly as a male red-backed shrike. His bluey-grey head was boldly marked with a black highwayman's mask over his eyes, and his peachy pink breast, his reddish-chestnut back and his long black and white tail made him very distinctive even to a novice bird-watcher as I was at the time.

The next year I saw my first female of the species. The females are duller in colouring – mainly a tawny brown above but nicely marked on the breast with small brown chevrons – and much more shy. By this stage red-backed shrikes had become my favourite birds and, despite the fact that I've since spent many hours watching birds and have seen other dramatic and exciting species such as drake smews, wallcreepers and red-footed falcons, they have remained firmly my number ones!

Below: Male red-backed shrike

Above: Female shrike, tawny in colouring

A couple of hundred years ago red-backed shrikes were widespread in Britain and even common in some places. By 1960, however, there were only about 250 pairs left. By 1971 they had dropped to about 80 pairs and by 1980 there was only a handful left. Worse, they had vanished from the New Forest near my home and in 1982 I didn't see a shrike all summer. This was very upsetting but there was a natural explanation for it. Despite many theories drawn up to explain this decline, such as habitat loss, colder summers and drought in its African wintering haunts, the shrike's rarity is due to a natural range shift. That is, they are all moving eastwards across Europe and into Russia, just as some birds have moved westwards and now are common here where two hundred years ago they were never seen.

However, one group of very selfish and sick people have speeded up the shrike's decline considerably. In 1983 I went to East Anglia to help protect the last few pairs of shrikes from egg collectors. These people take all the eggs and keep them in dark drawers to gloat over, like the madmen they are. Because the shrikes have always been a ''favourite'' of theirs, they have suffered badly. Indeed, recently a man was caught with 39 clutches – nearly 200 shrikes' eggs – in his house, and another man boasts of having robbed three times this number. Anyway, no nest I have ever guarded since has been robbed and I have spent many hours daydreaming of hideous tortures to inflict on any egg collectors I might catch.

In 1986 I again went to Suffolk to see what I thought would be my last nesting British red-backed shrikes, which had been guarded by the RSPB and had reared two youngsters. Then in 1987 I received the great news that one last pair had returned to this same site. Well, I must confess nothing could stop me. I dropped everything and tore off to see them. What a fantastic sight! Male and female shrikes courting, nestbuilding, catching bees, perching on bush tops and really showing off to all the hundreds of birdwatchers that came to see them.

Because of the wretched egg collectors, we had to guard the nest 24 hours a day. The reward was superb, because in late July four young shrikelets were squawking about wildly in the bushes while their parents chased insects all day to feed the hungry brood. Filming them for *The Really Wild Show*, I had the same feeling of wonder I'd had all those years ago in 1976. In a little green thorn bush about 10 metres away, sat all six of the shrike family. KAA POWW! Now I'm going to spend all this winter hoping that this wasn't my last view of my favourite birds; red-backed shrikes, the little pastel bandits, pretty princes of English fields!

BY CHRIS PACKHAM

PANDA PAGE

WHERE TO FIND PANDAS IN CHINA

U S S R

MONGOLIA

CHINA

RIVER HUANG HE

PANDA LIVE IN THIS SMALL AREA

RIVER CHANG JIANG

NEPAL BHUTAN

INDIA

BANGLADESH

BURMA

VIETNAM

LAOS

THAILAND

PANDA FACTS

■ There are probably less than 1,000 wild pandas left in their native country of China.

■ Pandas used to be hunted, but that's now been stopped. Today the main threat to their survival is the destruction of the forests they live in. The Chinese government has set up twelve nature reserves for the pandas, but their numbers are still declining.

■ Pandas are solitary animals, and rarely meet one another.

■ Pandas don't hibernate.

■ Pandas feed almost exclusively on the leaves, stems and shoots of bamboo.

■ The flowering of the bamboo is another of the threats to the panda's survival. At regular intervals (from ten to over a hundred years, depending on the species), the bamboo plants flower over large areas and die. It takes the bamboo about one year to grow again from seed but it can take up to ten years before it can support a panda population. During this time the pandas have to move to other areas where the bamboo has not flowered. That didn't matter in the past, but now that there are only a few reserves, the pandas can't move about freely, and some may starve.

■ Adult giant pandas weigh between 75 and 110 kg.

■ Giant pandas Chia-Chia and Ching-Ching were a gift in 1974 from the Chinese government to the British government.

In 1980 the World Wildlife Fund and the People's Republic of China started a project to learn more about the giant panda and to ensure its conservation. A research centre was set up at Wolong in China, and Western and Chinese scientists worked together to find out as much about pandas as possible. Reserves were established and laws passed to protect the panda. In 1956, sixty-two starving pandas were rescued from the wild. Programmes were set up to breed pandas in zoos outside China. A baby panda was born in Madrid Zoo.

Despite all this, a "panda emergency" was declared in 1987. Forests where pandas lived were still being cut down, and people were disturbing the pandas inside their own reserves. The number of wild pandas is believed to have dropped by two hundred. In 1986, sixty-seven pandas were found dead in the wild. Most of them had died from starvation. The Duke of Edinburgh held a press conference pleading for more help and more money for pandas. "There is a great danger that wild pandas will become extinct in the twenty-first century," he said.

So even with all this knowledge and effort by scientists, the panda is still in danger. Today the panda's last stronghold is in the hills of the central Chinese provinces of Sichuan, Gansu and Shaanxi. It has nowhere else to go. Westward lie the rock and ice of the Tibetan plateau, where pandas have never lived. Eastward lie plains and people. The panda has its back against the wall.

THE (SECOND) BIGGEST

Terry goes monster-hunting in a Scottish loch. No, not after the Loch Ness monster, but after an animal that's even bigger than the great white shark in *Jaws*.

We were floating along at a gentle five knots down a beautiful Scottish loch. It was hot and sunny, peaceful and lonely – just the gurgle of water under the bows of our launch.

Everyone aboard was staring out through binoculars, because *The Really Wild Show* was out to film a monster fish – at 9 metres long, the second largest fish in the world. Eight pairs of eyes scanned the water around the boat. There was tension and excitement in the air because we knew conditions were perfect for our animal to come to the surface.

I saw it first. I was in the bows, and dead ahead of us appeared a triangular black fin. "Shark!"

The boat slowly overtook the shark, but because of the sunlight on the water I couldn't see the animal itself. Then, as the shark came right under the bows and I was almost looking straight down at it, the whole of the body came into view. I gasped.

It was massive. The dorsal fin had given no impression of its size. Now the whole animal seemed as big as a small submarine, the length of a double-decker bus. At the back was a huge vertical tail, and at the front the classic stub-shaped nose of the shark, sticking out over an enormous gaping mouth.

And then, without warning, it gave a mighty sweep of its huge tail which rocked the boat, and dived out of sight.

"Quick! Get in the water before we lose it!"

Were we mad, going swimming with a huge shark? In fact, no! Because this monster was docile. Far from being a man-eater, our shark wouldn't hurt anything bigger than a shrimp – it was a basking shark, a huge but harmless feeder on plankton, the microscopic animal life which, on hot summer days, comes to the surface in vast quantities. In order to feed, the basking shark simply swims slowly along with its mouth wide open, taking in food and water. It needs huge quantities of food to fuel its massive body – up to 4 kilograms an hour, every hour, just to give it the energy to swim.

Within two minutes, I was in the water with

FISH IN THE WORLD

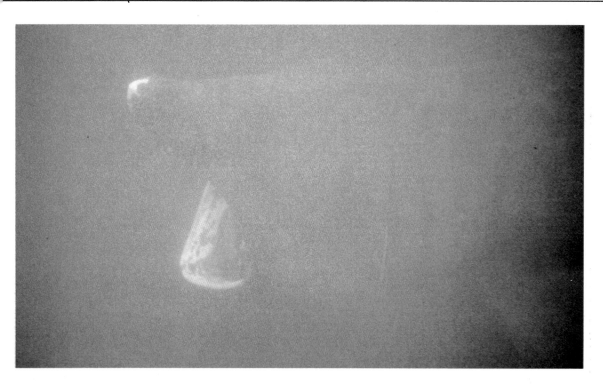

another diver behind the basking shark, and our inflatable launch had whisked two more divers around in front of it. Underwater cameras were switched on and, sure enough, it appeared before us.

As the shark became aware of us it simply turned off to one side, slipping noiselessly past us. But we had our shot safely in the camera, and as it glided past I kicked forward with my flippers, put out a hand and touched the body. Not smooth but rough, and scaly, like the bark of a tree.

Then it dived and, sadly, we saw it no more.

MYSTERIOUS SHARK TO YIELD ITS SECRETS . . .

The basking shark is one of several species which patrol the west coast of Britain! It's a mysterious animal because, although it's seen in summer, it seems to disappear in winter. At one time people thought it went into hibernation on the bottom of the ocean. Nowadays some scientists think it migrates northwards; others think the migration route isn't north at all, but south to African waters.

To answer questions like these, Dr Monty Priede, at Aberdeen University, designed a special radio transmitter that could be tracked by satellite. A transmitter was successfully attached to a shark in 1982. It stayed attached for 17 days.

The transmitter was towed by the animal. This meant the antenna was above the water whenever the animal was on or near the surface. The transmitter switched off automatically when it was completely under the water. Because of this, the satellite was able to detect when the shark was foraging on or near the surface.

In fact, Monty observed that the shark did not swim any great distance, and as a result, scientists like him are going back to the idea that basking sharks do, after all, go into some kind of hibernation.

"O.K. so what's the *biggest* fish in the world?"

The whale shark. Like the basking shark, it's also a plankton-eater. One was caught that measured over 12 metres, but there have been claims of whale sharks over 18 metres long.

Stephen the Chameleon

Nick with Stephen the chameleon. Stephen first came to the studio to help answer a question on how chameleons change colour, and soon become one of the regular presenters. He was to star with Ron in *The Really Wild Show Monster Movie*, and went on in the second series to demonstrate his amazing eyesight. Sadly Stephen died in 1987.

RON'S BIG NIGHT

The crowds outside Grosvenor House in London's Park Lane went wild as Ron arrived. Photographers and camera crews jostled and fought to get the best shots of Ron in his immaculate carrying-box. "Ron, look this way! Give us a big smile, Ron. Ron, do you think you're going to win the award?"

Ron played it cool. He said nothing but responded to the cheers with a wave of a rear leg. The crowds loved it. "Ro-on. Ro-on", they chanted. And, "Ron is red. Whales are blue. *Really Wild Show*, we love you!" Not a flicker of emotion crossed Ron's eight eyes, but inside, he was a seething cauldron of hopes and uncertainties. Would he, Ron, win the BAFTA award? Or, horror of horrors, would it go to ITV?

Inside the elegant dining hall, the other superstars cast admiring glances at Ron as he made his way to his table, firmly but politely refusing all requests for autographs. But he condescended to shake pedipalps with the BBC Governors and Controllers who queued up to pay their respects.

It was television's big night of the year when the British Academy awards, for the best programmes of the year, are presented. And the ceremony was being transmitted live on BBC 2. Ron absent-mindedly nibbled at a sautéed locust, as the minor awards for Best Drama of the Year, and Best Actor were presented. He knew that the real thrill of the evening would come with the announcement of the Best Children's Programmes.

As the tension-packed moment got closer, Ron felt himself go woozy. The rich food was playing havoc with his two stomachs; and the champagne was affecting his brain, which happened to be next to his stomachs, making him feel very queasy. During dinner, he'd noticed one or two bristles falling out of his sleek abdomen, and he'd had to brush them under the table hoping no one else had noticed. "Oh no," he thought, "I must have a moult coming on!" Yes, pre-moult tension was getting to Ron.

And so it was that, through a red haze, Ron saw a familiar face on the stage. He went weak in each of his eight knees. It was his favourite actress, Jane Asher, and she was announcing the nominations. Suddenly there he was on television! They were showing a clip from the very first edition of *The Really Wild Show* when Ron had walked on Marc Shedden's hand, and he'd said how "tickly" he felt. And then, a cameraman was beside the table, with his camera pointing at him, a spotlight blinding his eight eyes as he heard the words, "The winner of the Best Factual Children's Programme is . . . *The Really Wild Show*!" The applause was deafening. Ron tried to move, but the effort was too much. "Mike," he said to his tame producer, "you'd better go and pick up the award for me."

And so it was that the wrong person, a mere producer, was presented with the most important children's programme award of the year. "Very poor speech," said Ron. "Still, what can you expect from someone who's not an arthropod!"

PICTURE CREDITS

Photographs:
ARDEA pages 44 (Pat Morris) & 46 (M. D. England); BARNABY'S PICTURE LIBRARY page 33; MIKE BEYNON pages 52 & 57 *left*; BRITISH MUSEUM (NATURAL HISTORY) page 20 *bottom left*; B. CHRISTOPHER page 12 *bottom*; BRUCE COLEMAN pages 8–9 (Gunter Ziesler), 20 *bottom centre* (Frans Lanting) & *bottom right* (Hans Reinhard), 28 (Hans Reinhard), 29 (Hans Reinhard), 32 (Jane Burton), 38 *top* & *left* (*both* Hans Reinhard) & *bottom right* (R. Wilmshurst), 47 *right* (Dennis Green), 56 (Konrad Wothe) & 57 *right* (L. R. Dawson); JED EDGE page 37; SARA FORD page 39 *both*; GLOUCESTERSHIRE NEWSPAPERS LTD page 14; NATIONAL PORTRAIT GALLERY page 34; NHPA page 9 *bottom* (Stephen Dalton); OXFORD SCIENTIFIC FILMS pages 27 *bottom right* (Tim Shepherd) & 59; CHRIS PACKHAM pages 40 *top*, 41 *top* & 42 *both*; PLANET EARTH PICTURES pages 45 (Al Giddings), 47 *left* (John Lythgoe) & 55 (Nigel Downer); DR I. G. PRIEDE page 61; TIM RONEY pages 10, 17, 19, 20 *top*, 35, 40–41 *bottom*, 43, 60, 63 *inset* & 64.

Illustrations:
LINDEN ARTISTS: pages 16, 21, 34, 36 & 44; RAY & CORINNE BURROWS: pages 48–49 from *A New Look at the Dinosaurs* by Alan Charig, reproduced by permission of the British Museum (Natural History); KATE SIMPSON: pages 8, 9, 11, 32, 54 & 58.